Look Away Now

Poems of despair and hope

Lynn Michell and Rosie Pundick

2025
Linen Press

Published by Linen Press, London 2025

8 Maltings Lodge
Corney Reach Way
London W4 2TT
www.linen-press.com

Editors: Lynn Michell and Rosie Pundick.

Cover design: Lynn Michell
Cover image: Unsplash
Typeset by Blot Publishing –blot.co.uk
Printed by Lightning Source
ISBN: 978-1-0683417-3-1

How this began

Lynn Michell

At the end of 2024, I was struggling to know how to absorb and respond to what I had witnessed on my screen and on the news over the past year. It felt like a never-ending shock wave and a commentary on man's inhumanity to man.

Some friends stopped watching, so I asked myself what value was my nightly vigil in front of the television? Was it voyeurism to keep looking while more bodies were pulled from more rubble? The answer I gave myself was that the least I could do was stay informed so that I could sift the truth from the lies, as far as that was possible. I was aware too of compassion fatigue as never-ending bombs fell on civilians who were taking shelter and yet...each death, each act of brutality deserved to be noted. And mourned.

There was another all-consuming image, a bigger, all-pervading image of our planet under threat from our carelessness, our selfishness and our lack of action. It is overheated, losing species, heading perhaps for extinction. Soon.

Yet putting a finger on my own emotional pulse was pointless and helped no-one. What to do? I was thinking of protest and activism recorded for others to read. I was thinking of words which would say how it is and how afraid we are. And words which would offer hope. But I wrote nothing.

Instead I did what I could do - make a book and publish it. It would be a book of poems and short form prose that would record the many ways in which women are responding to being witnesses in these darkest times. I would ask my fellow writers to record their rage and anger, their placards and their marching. I would ask them to record small acts of kindness and compassion to ourselves, to each other, to those who suffer and to our planet. I wanted you to tell me how you went out in the rain and planted a tree.

In March 2025, we put out a call for poems. Some writers told us what I had said myself: I can't do this. How can I write about something this huge, this painful, this overwhelming? But others did. Over two-hundred-and-fifty pieces of writing came in. Each one was judged by a panel, and those that received a unanimous Yes went through to a short list and from there, most were accepted for publication in this anthology.

Many of those who submitted writing also thanked us for putting together women's voices that are louder together than separate, and which here record a communal cry of disbelief, anguish and fear. Amongst the sorrow and despair, you will find truth, courage and hope.

Safe Spaces

Avril Joy

—From Substack 03.07.2025

How do we carry on in times such as these when our news broadcasts and social media feeds are overwhelming? When our screens are dominated by angry old men and the immediate images of the wars they prosecute. When the reality of conflicts provokes anxiety and despair. When you find yourself shouting at the radio or the television. Weeping at the poignant, heartbreaking messages from Dr Ezzideen in Gaza[1] who *moves through the ruins, stitching wounds the world will never see.* And at night, writing *because some truths cannot remain buried.*

I am too easily drawn in. I am drawn in and away from the safe spaces that exist outside the news. I've been trying to find them, especially in the darker reaches of the night when I can't sleep and my phone is at hand. Phones should be banned at bedtime. Excuse: I use it as my clock. I need to get a clock!

These are some safe places where I've landed, each, as it happens, beginning with P.

POETRY

Poetry is essential to a writer's life. Jane Clarke writes of the landscape of the west of Ireland and the lives of its farming people. I'm drawn to the beauty of her lines, her storytelling, and the deceptive simplicity of her poetry. I am currently reading her debut collection *The River*. Elegant and lyrical, these poems evoke leaving and change. They speak of our continuing need to find a way to carry on and to endure.

PEONIES

Who doesn't love a blousy, frothy, pink peony? Who doesn't love a house full of peonies? A garden would of course be better, but as yet I've not grown them. My birthday comes when peonies are in season; this year, like others,
I have filled three vases with gifts of these early summer blooms.

---

[1] Dr Ezzidean writing on X, https://x.com/ezzingaza/status/1913356161631531348. 18th April 2025

POSTCARDS

I've been listening to The Shipping Postcards in which the Radio Four continuity team travel to some of the places in the *Shipping Forecast*. These brief, often touching pieces speak of safety and calm, of connection with home and the sea. What better litany to guard against a coming storm?

PROSE

Despite the horror of the news, or perhaps because of it, I need my own place of retreat and have begun a new novella to be written in prose of a fragmentary style. By 'begun' I don't mean the research, the thinking, the reading, but the actual writing – the first thousand words – saved in a file. More are drafted in my notebook. This landmark feels significant, a start after not knowing where to begin, the first stepping stones on a safe journey. I have given myself permission to walk this path of comfort and creativity. Continuing to create is a mark of quiet defiance, a refusal to be silenced or overwhelmed. I do not forget the tragic and brutal scenes playing out across borders far off. I carry them with me. I do not look away.

Contents

A Message

Jess Richards

You are going (softly) to get out of this (softly) put down your razor (softly) unclench your fingers (softly) leave your blood (softly) in your veins (softly) you will not always be inside (softly) this cold room with ice on the windowpanes (softly) with a television (softly) showing news (softly) showing who hates you (softly) showing who you hate (softly) screens and mirror-mirrors (softly) never show anyone's true self (softly) you will learn (softly) not to look at them too often (softly) especially when you have been hurt yet again (softly) the whole world's in a volatile state (softly) everywhere and everything is breaking (softly) you're thinking about glass shattering (softly) metal things (softly) falling all the way to hard ground (softly) assassination is tempting (softly) you don't have deadly skills (softly) don't know how to get a gun or fake passport (softly) your heroic mission (softly) bound to fail (softly) you have never been taught to kill (softly) not really the way out (softly) you are going to meet (softly) love (softly) to help you get out of this (softly) it will take many years—can't say how many but many (softly) when it feels like love (softly) you'll know it is love (softly) even when there's still nothing obviously gentle (softly) in this human world (softly) but one day alone (softly) sunshine reflects on snow (softly) you'll exhale your sharp edges (softly) away (softly) for once this will feel easy (softly) at the age of around sixty (softly) seventy, eighty, or ninety (softly) your hands will only touch soft things (softly) cat fur (softly) old blankets (softly) wrinkled skin (softly) threadbare towels (softly) thumbed pages (softly) curved flesh and worn sheets (softly) bathwater (softly) one day you'll smile (softly) quietly (softly) without a word (softly) you'll think—I got out and here there is love (softly) the other kind (softly) the kind love that loves you (softly) and this time you'll let it (softly) be soft.

History Judges Us, Too Late For Our Times

Kavita A. Jindal

The only way to live   is to not listen
                                   to desperation
Be it from far or near
Be it there or here
                                 Although
Sometimes you might want to set down your cup
Speak out   wade into an argument
talk facts and stats
talk drones, bombs, the return of stoning

Some days   the only way to live
might be to write, to speak,
                                 to not be shouted down
Perhaps lose some friends

A small loss for continuing in your comforts
but even your small gestures
                                 will gather force

History will judge too late
While the way to live   is to not listen
                                 to desperation.

Where Things Land

Nicole Gulotta

Dandelion, that weed—protruding
where the edge of the grass meets concrete.

Some are sprayed, ripped at the root. Others we pluck
and hold in front of our mouths, blow until each spore

has alighted, spitting and laughing on the last few
until they detach. Is this a kind of vengeance, growing

where it is unwanted? That weed is braver than me, surrendering
to the passersby, saddling its survival to the children, the lighthearted—

even the forlorn stop briefly for a small joy that might remind them
what it was like to be young. Always, we want to know

how it will turn out. If only we could see where things land.
But that's the bargain—not watching every seed sprout, even if we planted it

with our own two hands.

Nature is for Grieving

Jess Watts

Nature is for grieving;
It holds its dead as it holds its living
Gently,
I take my grief to the garden
Throw it up like a prayer that settles
Like a leaf, beside me.
I exist in it;
This existence is grief.
My footprints annihilate, even here
I tend to grief: I plant and reap –
Weep – alongside the heavens
That have opened up, for days now,
The bucket-pond on the patio is almost
Overflowing, I can see it from my bedroom window
The garden that has become my church:
A congregation of bees and sparrows, I
Weep – on the pew-steps that the bamboo
Has been fighting to uproot
For ten years now, a gardener has been over
Engaged in a futile war to hold the earth in place.
Now,
We've given up, given in, to grief, and someday
We will fill every crack with moss.

Nature is for grieving; I inhale
Its healing exhale; I lament
The destruction of my own.

The bee and I

Mare Heron Hake

the bee and I circle each other as I mow the lawn, as if I'd dropped a pebble in the pond of earth rounding my way around the we-planted tree, and I hear laughter over the loud machine and who cares that yes, it's for me, because around I will go around with the bee at my shoulder, wasp, a buzzer to warn I coming too close to the nest, yes, I nod, I'll move on, keep going, a labyrinth, and another, knitting the house to the yard, to the fence, this yard to the neighbor's, the bee flies across us all, so false the boundary of what we think we own, the land, the nest, the high ground, the rage this week as some are arrested, the blood as others die with their families, or after them, do we own our blood, do we own our anger alone, see the neighbor waves to me with pesticide in his hand, thinking the bee will not sip but of course she will, and around I walk, wondering if I can lay white beach stones at the flower's edge, like water lapping the shore, rounded stones to soften that sad line. someday, an owner of this house may cut down the we-planted tree because it is too small, too in-the-way, not-the-right-type, and I won't be here to protect it. nurtured from seed, it will die in the only yard it has ever known, a life lived in my circles, a life at the center of where I walk, the bee and I, above the boundaries others would have us make walk around the tree, letting the circle go wider, where the grass becomes shorter, and the wildflowers called weed still thrive.

Garden

For JHG and NHG on their wedding. Love is love.

Khadija Rouf

Its design is a living map, of places travelled, of many plants tapestried with care,
Seeds grow, remembering castle walls, salt marshes, crows threading inky skies,
Now roots are woven into footholds in brickwork or shade nested or drinking sunlight,
Here, where the fox once lurked, is frothing penny wort. Grape vines twist around pergolas,
wild garlic bursts into stars, making crisp heat on our tongues,
The meals eaten here: breaking bread, eating flowers, drinking wine.

Within these seasoned walls, fur, fin and feathers flourish between the green.
Each spring, the snow bird arrives like a celestial stranger, seeking shelter,
Finches thrum, wings cresting amidst roses ascending the walls, all white petals and thorns,
Sparrows chatter in the guttering, where sapphire eyes are watching,
and occasionally, a pale velvet paw jabs hopefully at the eaves,
In summer, litters of mirabelles splash through the canopy, soft drumming
making way for the rhythm of autumn, the falling of leaves,
Golden fish observe the fractured world above their heads, rippling silently,
Their exhaling breaks the meniscus like bubbles in champagne,
Until, sparkling cobwebs adorn winter branches and mulberry roots bury themselves,
deep, deep in the soil. All our roots entangle here, underneath our feet.

After storms, a raindrop slides the length of an olive branch
pearling at its tip; an orb which turns this world upside down
splits the light into rainbows
shining into *this* Eden, illuminating *this* love,
Blessing lips upon lips, hearts within hearts.

Anchorless in the Light

Andrena Zawinski

*...and in that veil of light/the city drifts /
anchorless / upon the ocean.* —Lawrence Ferlinghetti

It starts this way each morning—house wrens
flirting potato vines, spray of sea on sand,
then the crows and their warnings, mornings
dewy under sun. Come step onto the porch,

the view no longer blocked by the diseased pine.
We have this the gift of water beyond the marina,
its rocky channel gateway to a smooth bay.
Listen to buoys singing with wind in the fog,

old tug announcing its entry against the bark of a seal,
swoop of pelican wings. Linger here in this veil
of white light blinding with beauty, reminding
to hold onto this, hold it close and dear

no longer stuck inside glass and brick, sight set
on neighboring chatter, the drunken songs and brawls,
all of it weedy with ivy, bats circling chimneys,
unlike these distant hills yet to be peopled. But last night

in a dream their mounds became an unlit stretch of halls,
splintered doors on every wall, dust motes flecking air
over muddy cliffs where nothing stirred, except a parade
of dead who nodded, waved, winked, then dissipated,

the heart pounding, but here in this new day we can moor
and watch with steadied breath the rise of light. Come here.
Stay close, make this watch and listen to the lilt
of the mourning dove's coo, anchorless in the light.

The Hunger of Fish

Sally J. Morgan

In this photograph with curled corners, is a woman on the shore of a foreign land disguised as home. One side of the beach lies under brown cloud piled in layered thicknesses over gun-grey water, the other is all sunlight and ochre shadows spilling towards the sharp line where the rain stops.

The woman stands with a foot on either side of the divide. One cheek wet with the rain falling as soft as powdered salt, the other burning in the stark southern hemisphere sun. Dogs run in and out of the water, birds and fish swirl above and below, a man casts out into the waves, his lead sinker flashing like the kahawai he wants to catch. The sound of his reeling line meshes with the cries of New Zealand gulls, whose voices are so much more urgent than those British ones she knew and will know again. They dive on his bait as it hits the water.

This woman is me: emigrant, immigrant, now home-returner—holding a photograph.

Standing outside of myself in a place that I loved but never loved me, feeling the shifting of tectonic plates and the coming of cyclones.
My eye follows the line of mountains and islands that link through land and sea. Volcanoes. Some living. Some dead. Lava moves under us all the time. Heat unfelt and venting in a pillar of smoke.

Once I was in a chartered motor-dinghy, anchored off a tiny obsidian islet where sulphur crusted the edge and the smell of rotten eggs steamed from its bubbling centre. The water was warm and filled with fish. I caught a silvered trevally on the hook that I'd baited with the flesh of its kin. Its siblings were ravenous. Their violence furrowed the lava-warm water, boiling the surface and bending my rod until the line screeched.

There is ash in the sky somewhere over there.
And out to sea, fishes swarm around the black-glass rocks.
Eating their own.

Resurrected she returns

Regi Claire

Resurrected she returns, her apron full of see-through pears or cherries
from another season. The stairwell climbs in air and so does she, up and up

towards the memory of her kitchen's dazzle. Slowly as she moves she
reinstates the steps, one, then two, then three, a flight and turn and here it is,

the essence of her home, here in a few feather flicks of a bird as it descends,
circles once and spiral-shimmers off into the open blue of what's to come.

Things in the fridge

Mona Dash

There are things rotting in the fridge
the yoghurt we bought some days ago
our footsteps loud in the quiet superstore
angry our eyes, enraged our voices, as we seethed
about the news in the papers; the kisses
not shared for years coiling in that anger
you agreed with some, I disagreed with some
never the same things, and our footsteps grew angrier
as we argued louder, louder, the echoes lodging
in the yoghurt, now watery, large flecks of green mould
decorating its whiteness. It has gone off
as has this, this packet of beansprouts, healthy food
bought the day the fires raged
humans howled and animals cried human tears
there's ash, broken bits of bones in the sprouts
and this meat, delicate-pink, we had bought the morning
they broke god's own house and danced on its ruins
as they have been doing for centuries
used drones over cities and maimed the children
the meat now mould-green, saffron, the smell drowns
the citrus deodorant in the fridge, and this Philadelphia
bought yesterday at news-time, as leaders spoke,
has sprouted large green spores on its soft cream cheese body
the leaders, from countries, where we live, where we love
where we were born, where we holiday, they talk louder
the acquiesced gather, the applause gets stronger
the narrative the same, the hate the same, and the voices all together
rise so high, so fast, and escape out of windows
over the houses and sweep, sweep across
those crimson skies, those drying rivers, those sinking mountains
and here in the fridge, more and more things rot.

Watching Perfume Ads with the Sound Off

Jess Richards

He looks at her / getting onto a plane / his lips are parted / she turns / glares at him / disappears / in a train carriage / he jumps / over many people / he's wearing thermal underwear / she's escaped / a cage / she's in a bed / she's in a desert / she's outside in the grandest courtyard / she kisses men with no shirts on / these are farmers / picking grapes / it's backbreaking work / a man arrives / his white shirt is clean / he's running / between grapevines / getting no dirt on himself at all / a man and a woman kiss / she runs along a beach / he drives a car along the same beach / not crashing into her / she turns / her hair is a cloud / she says a thin word / he can't lipread a woman in a wide green dress / now she's dancing like a lemur / in front of an enormous mirror / another woman dressed in gold / eats chocolate / pours chocolate / shouts something / no one hears / she runs away / she punches a man / brown eyes dissolve into the ocean / a woman chases birds away from herself / in another desert / a rich man sneaks up on a rich woman / she acts like she doesn't know he's there / two sailor men (might be girls) pretend to be boys / almost or not quite in love / circle around the heads of yet another man and woman / distance is usual / he breathes on the gap / between her lips and breakable neck / coiled with ivory and adders / sand colours the sky in / another aeroplane / a woman gets into a yellow bath / tall indoor ferns / water drips from her skin / she's not even wet / is that glue?

No one in a perfume ad ever experiences winter / no one is on a waiting list / no one has greys or wrinkles / switches on a kettle / no one in a perfume ad / lives in a street of terraced houses / no one lights fires / plants bulbs for next spring / shoplifts nappies / cries / comes home late / doesn't come home at all / no one votes and hopes for something to change / dreams of deep lakes / no one in a perfume ad / hangs out the washing / saves a crow from drowning in the canal / buys chips without fish / chats to snails / closes a credit card account / adopts a stray and toothless cat / no one in a perfume ad / repairs a cracked wall / calls their confused mum / finds someone's bank card and cuts it up / watches a murmuration of starlings / lays flowers for Dad / turns the thermostat down / no one leans in a doorway / smells soil after rain / checks on quiet neighbours / kisses their spouse / shares spare cabbages around / walks dogs beside a brown river / picks blackberries at the edge of the dual carriageway / counts bees and worries / knocks on a door for help / No one in a perfume ad watches rainclouds clearing / darns woollen socks / waits for the sparrows to hatch in the air-vent / gets a new job / boil-washes dishcloths / suffers identity theft / cooks a fry-up from leftovers / finds an old book of stamps / asks awkward questions / dances around their kitchen to four a.m. radio songs / No one in a perfume ad prays for a cooler summer next year / the next year / the next / is there nothing here to envy?

Departure Time

S.J. Litherland

The dream was departing taking its ragged edges into the sea
snatches of voices like seagulls crying.
I awoke and in my head the day started, early morning late autumn.
I said aloud: *Moments of unreality colliding.*
A phrase needed for the final poem to be dispatched.
I was sitting in the train of departure in the station. The train
shunting back and forth on branch lines of possible outcomes
each one fading as I sat with pencil or with pen
or at the computer. It was the final poem of last words
to the earth and to grandsons, superseded by last thoughts

not yet composed. I was sitting looking out of the window,
drawing a blank as they say, as if there is a blank page
that looks back at you. Like the unconscious with no words,
the mixing of all meanings in a swirl
until the brain came waving its note at the window, processed and ready.
The willing worker on the night shift.
I looked up Eliot: *human kind cannot bear very much reality.*
Burnt Norton, Little Gidding, The Dry Salvages, East Coker,
like stops on the line, a sermon on a high plain above the floodwater.
And I saw the present colliding with the future.

Clean

Jess Watts

Crouched over the earth the child draws lines with a stick as the ancestors had done. A second child, more cautious, more weighted by unease — a conscience, possibly — watches on. The first child divides the soil cleanly. A clean disregard. "This is where I'll build the house." A school project, all the children are called to build a house in miniature. "But what about the ants?" asks the second child, and points a pale finger at black scrambling bodies. The first child looks up. "They're *ants*."

Fireweed

Rebecca Faulkner

On the 26th night of bombardment I shake
the stench of gas from brocade curtains

wipe brick dust from porcelain
contemplate gingerbread baked without eggs

      at the all-clear
every stem in the garden has its neck broken

from the safety of the patio we watch
the evening shuffle in a nightgown dances

in the hedgerow   poplars painted pitch black
      I want to tell you about your son

his freckles the color of burnt straw
about fireweed crouched in the dust of the dead

      their magenta spires resolute
nudging cracks in next door's fence

but there is no more room inside your busted skull for us

only silence and burning fuselage
      on the far edge of an ocean

your feet crumpled against the cockpit
as the air empties   I watch weeds lay low

their roots breathe in and out
while I light the stove

Michaelmas Daisies

Gillie Griffin

Purple asters are blooming in the garden,
in time to celebrate the feast of St Michael,
and all angels.
Although no-one does anymore.
The last days of harvest. All is gathered in.
Blackberries soured by archangel spit.

Tiny purple explosions from a golden centre.
Too many heads to count on one plant.
Safe in my garden
I want only to write of my flowers,
my head filled with bombs,
endlessly falling on Gaza. Too many bodies
to count. Women, children, men who want only
to tend their gardens, harvest their fruit in peace.

Michaelmas daisies lined the nave of my childhood church,
tucked in umbrella stands at the end of each pew.
Their scent: notes of balsam and dirty socks
released by the brush of choristers' cassocks,
processing blindly behind the crucifer.

Onward Christian soldiers, marching as to war,
with the smell of bad eggs and marzipan
hanging thick in the air; the stench of rotting flesh.

Outside in my garden asters sparkle
by torchlight. Hundreds of purple stars,
dust motes in the wilderness.

Mikail, angel of mercy, where are you now?
Michael, protector of the innocent, where are you?

Thirsty

Laura Bissell

I can't drink Diet Coke anymore because it violates Palestinian human rights
and aspartame causes cancer
can't drink milk because it's the sustenance produced for another mammal's infant
and because of climate change

I can't drink almond milk as it takes 130 pints of water to make one glass
described as 'sending bees to war'
can't drink coconut milk as global demand has led to deforestation
and exploitation of workers

I can't drink rice milk as it's a water hog belching greenhouse gas
can't drink soy as the Amazon rainforests are alight
I can't drink bottled water because there are more plastic bottles in the sea than fish
whales stomachs full of it

can't drink coffee because conventional trade traditionally discriminates against
agricultural
communities in low-income countries
and it keeps me up at night

I can't drink tea, because of child labour, poor wages, and a bitter aftertaste of
colonialism
can't drink juice, not just the air miles but the tooth rot,
and I can't stomach drinking from a metal straw now plastic straws are cancelled

I can't drink kombucha as I don't want to get done for drink driving
can't drink hot chocolate: see reasons for coffee
I can't drink Irn Bru because it looks radioactive and because they changed the recipe

I try water straight from the tap
and pray for those in Flint, Michigan
the day I decided I hated Obama with his performative sip

I am dangerously dehydrated
thirsty and thirsting
arid and parched
I could drink a lake, a loch, a reservoir, a stream, a river, a brook,

I could drink water straight from a spring coming out of a mountain, if I didn't
have to drive my
car to get there

I am thirsty
What should I drink?

We drink, dance and f***

Regi Claire

We drink, dance and f*** while in the next room tower blocks explode
with the sound turned down; while still-warm bedclothes ignite
into cindered settling dust

and pink-red blossom is blown across –

wedding confetti for the world to come where our shadows,
always grey, always absurd, will pass harmlessly over the earth,
over grass and tree roots erupting from shattered bone.

When I say I live in the moment it's not a brag

Abigail Thomas

Time makes no sense. Whole decades vanish without my noticing. Where do they go? Thankfully I am at home in the present. I think of each moment as a nautical swell, and I ride one after another and almost never wipe out. Some moments are longer than others, some steeper. But I can carry on a reasonable conversation, make a birthday cake, get to the bathroom, feed the dogs. I can make things out of clay, unless I run out of it. If I keep my wits about me, I can handle whatever shows up in the present, but mention something interesting that happened recently and it's a different story. My daughter referred to a conversation we had had the day before, and I drew a blank. I am used to things slipping my mind, but not quite so quickly. This lapse frightened me, and I said as much. She tried to comfort me, talking about how stress affects everything, and how long I've lived, how much to remember already, and she calmed me down. I am beginning to accept that each day is a day unto itself, there's no guarantee how much of Friday will survive the trip into Saturday. So the present is all I've got, or at least all I'm certain of. Luckily, each moment holds a world.

Lighthouse

Ellen Bass

It's late and I'm pushing the baby in the stroller
through Lighthouse Field.
The grasses give off the damp straw smell of darkness coming on.
Walk, the baby commands.
So I unbuckle the strap and set her down.
It's February first and the ground's still swollen
from the atmospheric rivers that flooded California.
We were up till four in the morning,
with sump pumps and sand bags, schlepping
every sopping towel and blanket and bathrobe,
while the baby slept in her crib.
There are no cars here in the field
so she can have a little sovereignty
as she wanders behind me. And faintly,
I hear her singing to herself,
Twinkle Twinkle.
The whole song. *Like diamond sky.*
She's almost two. I'm seventy-five.
I won't be here when the worst
of what's coming comes. I think about it
and then I try not to think about it.
And then I try to think
because if we don't—but I can hardly grasp it.
I mean her in it. The tiny glint of her voice.
Something starts to collapse.
Love and dread are brethren
said a mystic woman in the Middle Ages.
For a moment the sun
reclines on the bare branches of the maples.
They're rinsed with gold.
And then the light is gone. The tree is itself again.
It's time to return the baby to her father.
The long beam of the lighthouse strobes the path.
I put her in the stroller and start walking fast.

Narrow Gauge

Rachel Burns

After a night of snow, I walk around the blue frozen lake,
swans huddle in the corner. I meet a woman,
familiar, yet I can't place her.

Faces escape me, perhaps I've met her before,
before the small oaks planted in the hope of a wood,
before the viaduct was fenced off with two metal gates,
one spray painted with a Lakota chief; arms outstretched.

I remember once you had to walk past wild horses.
Pigs in pens. Now the feeding wheels are rolled to the side,
barbed wire snipped away; footpath overgrown
with moss & fireweed, brambles & fern.

The viaduct stretching across the River Wear,
walkway covered in saplings & giant hogweed.
Sycamores deeply rooted in the narrow gauge.
Samaritan calling cards pinned to railings.

It's a long way down, it would be so easy, yet.
Come, I say, to the woman, tread carefully, take your time.
She squeezes my arm.   Hun, let's go back. I hesitate

but then a grey heron, wings outstretched,
takes off from the viaduct, lands below the arch spans,
easy and grey as a flat pebble, skimming the mouth of the river.

Spotting a Splash of Red (on my walk)

Joan Leotta

Around the opposite side of the pond,
amid a copious swath of green leaves
a single splash of red poked out.

Curious, but tired from my walk
I decided it was simply some sort of rose,
turned, then, curiosity won out and I circled

round to the flower's place, where I
discovered a full-in-bloom, red canna lily,
bent by wind or an animal, so that instead of

standing tall and straight with its fellows in
that mass of leafy green tongues, that bent stem
left this blossom's colors barely peeking out

from among those surrounding leaves.
I realized suddenly that I am that very flower,
a bit broken by time's winds and hard pushes,

not able to stand as tall and straight as when young,
but still, even broken, bent, with words and love,
I can still bloom in beauty, bright and red, if I will.

Laundry

Ellen Bass

The baby's dragged the sheets to the kitchen
and now she's stuffing them in the washer,
one hand lifting a wad of yellow cotton,
the other reaching down for more and more. Breathing heavy,
she's feeding vast swaths by the armful,
bent halfway into the mouth of the machine,
a strip of skin exposed where her shirt's ridden up,
an edge of diaper sticking out of her pants.
Who can watch a child and not feel fear
like static in the background or a tinnitus you try to ignore.
This morning, in the *Times*, I saw the galaxy LEDA 2046648—
each spiral arm distinct and bright against the dark ink. Light
from a billion years ago, just as the first
multicellular life emerged on Earth.
What are the not-quite-two years of this intent creature
in the sweep of time? Her quadriceps and scapula,
the alveoli of her lungs, twenty-seven bones of her hand
that evolved from the fin of an ancient fish.
And her scribbly hair sticking up from her first pony tail.
When she was in her mother's body,
the California fires turned the air a smoky topaz
and the sun glowed orange on the kitchen wall.
Last month the floodwaters rose and seeped under the door.
Still, there must be time for this, to watch her—
hands deep into the doing, she's wedded
to the things of this world.
When she stands, her sleeve slips down
and she pushes it up like any woman at work.

A Lesson in Disorder

S.J. Litherland

A blue glass vase   on a glass table   held a decaying
bunch of rosemary.   I liked its disarray.   half broken
stems. Cut from the herb patch.   jammed into a blue vase

without ceremony or arrangement.   It looked
unremittently wild.   A bunch breaking all the rules.

Then my jacket caught the edge of it.   It was swept
in its needle lattice onto the floor.   I imagine a wasps nest.

How could I rearrange its wildness? I had to remove each spear.
Pointing the right way   upwards.   Bits of this and that.
Assembled with disorder in mind.   It looked so balanced.

Every stem a history of placing.   A lesson in time.
It was too well adjusted.   The poetry   left on the floor.

Atmospheric Rain

Connie Hills

Rain's wet feathers fall on
early mauve magnolia blossoms.

A grove of shimmering redwoods
pronounce this land sacred

as university students scurry
behind window walls where

a woman of science tells you:
 "Your retina cells are dying."

Something you already know
as unlit rooms & dark streets

become grey gauzy film noirs
with swift moving characters.

You sidewind through slush
in the blurry night to find shelter

at Tacos Oscar. Rivers of rain
drumbeat the aluminum roof.

Across the black patio garlands
of tiny white lights glisten on walls

heat lamps spark like fireflies
over the French Broad River.

Above a flickering votive
your wife's eyes birth two new stars.

Warm cumin rises from paper
plates of chicken tinga tacos.

Comfort food, kitchen gods,
smoky chiles of surrender.

Tonight, in your dimly lit universe
nothing is shy of enchantment.

Here in the winter light

Mara Gale Fein

Now I am old enough to understand
people speaking of God
as though he was known to exist
like a delivery man

who would visit and take orders
the deus ex machina of happy endings.
They no doubt believed
in him like Edison or Morse
just a light or a knock-on wood away.

It is hard to give thought to such things
after appointment books of pain
meals of condolence.
So much depends upon
the light of your soul
hobbling the darkness of
the silent room
the words never spoken
the still life
and you
pentimento
lost beneath a prayer.

This is not a time for war

Regi Claire

we buried part of you

one year ago to the day
day of the dead
all the dead everywhere

cease–
ground is taken hostage
                    –fire

stars devastated in shot silk

cease–
bodies fight losing battles
                    –fire

rituals of candles
anthems of the long gone
hot held hands

The Storm Woke Us

Carol McKay

1968. The storm woke us, rocking
the innermost floorboards of our flat as if
it could dismantle them, might dismantle them,
we didn't know, and we were walking on them,
grasping the impermanence of what
we'd assumed was solid.

> *Innocent*
> *as a child in a war zone fleeing bombing*
> *in a wooden cart drawn by a donkey,*
> *lines of light appearing and disappearing*
> *between the base planks, shifting*
> *with the road's uncertain camber.*

I was newly turned twelve when the hurricane
killed twenty-one people in Glasgow.
Chimneys toppled through slate roofs.
Gable ends crumpled to pavements.
Tiles crashed from the tops of high tenements,
fracturing like shrapnel.

2025. This new building quakes
in the harsh blasts haranguing it. Beyond the window,
the huge crane, taller than the 1960s high-rise
it was built to disassemble, sways in the wind,
seeming brittle. On the birches on the slope
where there were houses, the magpies' nest remains
glued in place though trees fold and straighten.

> *TV is screening the war aftermath:*
> *They're reporting sixty thousand killed in Gaza.*
> *Concrete dust clads people, streets and olive groves.*

In the storm aftermath, footpaths are strewn
with damp twigs, lichened branches, bin litter.
Leaf-mould on the pavement becomes a prayer rug,
patterned with a scattering of scarlet –

berries from the shrubs in council gardens.
One, translucent as a prayer bead,
gleams against the tree's blackened trunk.

Finding a prayer

Mona Dash

If this disheartens, the news heavy with statistics
of deaths, of the unwell, of inept governments getting it wrong
the delicate balance between people and wealth creation
hoping the ozone layer is healing, though the cries of humans keep rising
and if this relieves; seeing a flash of a rainbow strung high up there
hearing a song of the bird you have never seen before
walking alone along little streams, feet firm on wet earth
think back then, sweeping history, what mankind has done, and been through
the wars, the disasters, the anger, the hatred, we have killed and maimed
explored and invented, served and sacrificed, we have sung, we have loved
we have sunk in gutters, swum across rivers, we have survived, we have lived
look back then and find the hope.

Word a prayer
           hold it
                  call it your own.

Linen chests

Lindsay Kellar-Madsen

For the child carried in a bath towel, through bombed-out streets of Lviv.

Instead,
> I make you a sandwich.
> Sliced apple grins snuggle neat seams

of bread
> and we whisper where the wild grows fat
> with raspberry thumbs in the yard. They climb

beside a sprawling quilt
> of bluebells. Today, you will see no wolves, no
> cloud is a hungry jaw of teeth. We floss grassy toes

in a frothing sink.
> Later, you sleep—hammocked and lost to a knot
> of dreams. When the heavy pendulum swings,

your body
> between blue plum trees, your mother and I
> pour strong coffee. Because women will swallow

a whole fortress
> of secrets, while old men haunt our closets. Unravelling, we name
> the bodies and drown enemies in fabric softener. We swap scraps

of wisdom—
> how to stratify lupin seeds cold in the fridge,
> how long to soak blood stains in salt water.

Etiquette for our Tormentors

Susan Brady Konig

"Baby ducks cannot survive without their mother. They are helpless."

My sister is reading off the internet about wood ducks. "What eats baby ducks?" she's Googling. "There is a lot here," her brow furrows. "They shouldn't be alone."

We sit in Adirondack chairs by the fast-moving stream in back of her house, two women born in the 1960s, now in our 60s, watching two young ducks trying to swim upstream against small waterfalls and slippery rocks without the ability to fly. I'm impressed. "Look, they are doing great." They pause in a still pool and face each other making a little heart-shaped silhouette of their bodies. "And they have each other," I point out.

"Where's their mother?" she agonizes.

They keep hopping and swimming until they are out of sight. "They'll be fine," I say.

But one of the ducks, caught in the current, comes tumbling downstream and over the little waterfall, carried back down to where it started. Alone.

"Oh no," she says.

"Look," I say, "it's already starting back up. It'll catch up with its sibling." It hops, it swims. My sister twists her shirttail in her fingers. "You will never catch it," I say, as she eyes the stream and the slippery docks. I'm already imagining the emergency room visit.

"I know," she sighs. "The internet says it takes five people to catch a duck." The duckling seems tired and starts cheeping. "It's crying!"

"It's communicating. They'll hear each other," I say.

"Every predator in the woods will hear the distress and eat that baby," she says. "I'd almost rather a hawk come and take it right now. It's so sad. All they had was each other."

The duck continues to struggle upstream until it's dark and we can't see or hear it anymore. "It'll be okay."

My sister doesn't sleep. At 6 am she wraps a hot water bottle in a towel and places it in a reusable shopping bag. She dons binoculars and a headlamp and starts walking upstream in her Converse sneakers because she doesn't want to scare ducks in more appropriate, safer wading boots.

Like Spiderman's grandmother, making three points of contact on the mossy rocks and boulders and slippery pebbles and logs beneath the water, she travels upstream in search of ducklings, duck cadavers, signs of bloody violence. Any answers or clues. She makes it as far as a bridge where a trail crosses the stream. She climbs out of the water and walks back home by the road.

Later we are back by the stream discussing our late mother and what might have caused her to be narcissistically wounded. Finally, I'm not sure why, after fifty years, I tell my sister that one of our relatives molested me when I was 10.

I can see the panic in her face. How is she going to react and instantly repair this secret that has taken me decades to share. She is the fixer. Should she wear boots or sneakers?

He's dead, and I don't care anymore, I tell her. What I do care about is why our damaged parents consistently exposed us to this strange and violent man throughout our childhoods.

What is the etiquette of the tormented toward their tormentors? When does bad get bad enough to call time out? I knew it was wrong, but I didn't know why. I never told our parents.

"He was at my wedding," my sister says.

"I know," I say.

"You went to his funeral."

"And didn't shed a tear."

We hear a cheep.

"Is that a duck?" my sister asks. The two siblings are there together in a quiet pool by the mossy bank of the stream. They are dabbling, a dunking motion that means they know how to feed themselves. They have feathers, not down. They will soon fly, and they have each other. "I'm so happy I could die right now," she is crying.

"See, I told you it would be okay."

Our parents were not there for us, but we had each other. We tumbled over the rocks, and we survived.

Weather Patterns

Beth Oast Williams

If you believe a single
flutter of a butterfly wing
can cause a typhoon,
you might have dreams
the gods are in us all,
dust from the big bang
glue to our bones
and hinges. One gun
points out a window
at the driver
of another moving car.
We call it a traffic
disruption, all of us
slowing down to take
a look, the rear view
mirror a mere whisper
to the coming storm.

Pull Towards The Edges Of Earth

Sue Moules

Sea crashes against stone and houses
erodes the beach
pulls further inland
I know I need to hold you by the hand
and take you with me.

We only have this life
time has eroded most of it,
now we must turn and move
the tide is coming in,
we must run toward it
watch the sun drown beneath
its depths
breathe in the boundary.

Weathering the Storm

Rachel Burns

We are glossing doors and stairs, skirting boards,
everything in brilliant white. Outside the storm topples trees,

blows over an entire pier in Llandudno,
where my grandfather once painted the white hotels in Great Orme.

I scroll my newsfeed; *Japan aquarium cheers up lonely sunfish*
by taping photos of human faces to its tanks. I have stopped taking

those little white pills that fog the brain.
Last Tuesday, I watched Finn paint a blackbird in the snow.

As he painted the blue wash, each drop of berry red in the snow,
each branch of willow. The blackbird, yellow beak, soft brown feathers.

Once the storm passes, I tidy the dust sheets, soak the brushes in turpentine,
and walk around the nature reserve, tracing the lake in a figure of eight,

stepping over sycamore limbs, branches scattered like chess pieces.
There is a light dusting of white feathers, swans unscathed,

capsized like boats, as they feed off the bottom of the lake.

Suicide des Oiseaux: The Apocalypse

Alexis Rhone Fancher

1.

6 AM. Something winged kamikazes our glass front door, looking for a way in. *It's a bad omen*, I tell my spouse. *No. It's a shrike*, Jimmy says, holding the dead bird by its feet. *I looked it up on line.* He's got an answer for everything.

They've swarmed the 30 ft. tall, silky oak in the front yard, its yellow blossoms a seed depository; for the shrikes, a tasty meal. I watch them gather round. The tree shivers like I do when Jimmy's mad and takes it out on me.

Again. That sharp crack! Like a rock, thrown at the skylight, or a twig, snapped beneath my boot. I look out at the shiny morning. *Maybe it's something else this time*, I say. *Babe*, Jimmy says, his voice shrill. *It's just another suicidal bird!* He tolerates no dissent.

By the time he leaves for his poker game, it's sunset. I watch as shrikes hurl themselves at the reflected glare, their vision obscured, their imagined nirvana instead a cruel trompe l'oeil. Sweet birds! Don't they know it's worse on the inside? What do they hope to find on this side of the glass?

2.

I don't know why you're so upset, my spouse says after dinner. I take his hand and lead him to to the atrium. Six dead shrikes, lined up like sacrifice. *What does this mean?* I ask. Jimmy smirks, rolls his eyes. *Maybe it's the beginning of that apocalypse you keep talking about?*

This morning: A roadrunner dive bombs the skylight. The silky oak, its launch pad. Has the roadrunner been watching the shrikes, wondering what's the attraction? Decides to find out for itself. Splat! Smash! Maybe it's a warning. A cautionary tale.

On our grocery list for today: Breakfast. Eggs. Bacon. Yukon Gold potatoes, a soupçon of compassion, over easy, hash browns on the side. When Jimmy hasn't returned by midnight, I grow worried. Call him. Text. No answer. *It's a game*, he laughs when he finally returns. *Did ya miss me?*

Last night's dream: That's me, the shrike, dive bombing the high windows, desperate for a way out.

Pale Blue Vein
November 2023

Ellen Bass

The count of the dead
in Gaza is rising. Last
night 15,000, 6,000 children.
It could be me
there with a dead baby. No one
decreed I'd be born
in a row house in Philadelphia.
No one wrote in the Book of Life
that my father would escape
the pogroms, carried
on his brother's shoulders
through the snow from Kiev to the sea.
There was a time
I thought the pain of the *other*
was not like my pain.
Every five minutes a child dies in Gaza.
It could be our baby.
Her eyebrow, its perfect arc,
the pale blue vein
that sweeps out
from the tip of her brow,
as though some lesser god
gave up on the rest
of the world and in her idleness just
added this extra touch
of beauty to beauty.

How to Quilt a Peace

Avril Joy

I can promise you that women working together...can bring peace and prosperity to this forsaken planet. —Isabel Allende

Start small, begin with what can be salvaged, in Gaza
a man buys back his stolen coat, a dog named Hope
rehomed. Do not chase a gold Medallion five-pointed star
or chalk a sober Amish diamond in a square. But pin
a patchwork of fat quarters appliquéd in a child's face,
missing limb, drone, orphan, beggar in the ruins. 'Why
is he begging' she asks on the South Bank all those years
ago in '74. 'He's dodging the draft' I say sleeping
on a stranger's floor, a graveyard quilt, litter of flightless
birds anointed in orange.

Frame a Bargello in turkey red,
border in black grouse on the road to Baghdad, a thousand
pink flamingos at rest on the front line near Kherson.
Cover him. Muffle the voice at the gates of Auschwitz.
Quiet the parrots roosting on the Eiffel Tower warning of
incoming fire. Put away steel, wax thread, banish men,
block instead a Birds of the Air. Leave and feather a North Country
quilt, bind a lover's knot single fabric wholecloth patterned
in fleur-de-lys. Piece by hand, stitch by women's parloured hand.
In stone cold cottages by candlelight begin again.

A Graveyard in the New World

Sally J. Morgan

Boston is full of graveyards: joyless but beautiful places, light-blocked by tall buildings and filled to their edges
with stooped trees and dead puritans. I wander through the crowded rows of the King's Chapel Burying
Ground with my head down, thin daylight breaking through the hard-leaved trees to run over my shoes in
rippling patches the size of coins. The contrast between the blue of the sky up above and this shadowed cube
of cellar-like darkness is theatrical. Stubby, hand-carved gravestones on either side of me are topped with
winged-skulls like children's drawings, and their seventeenth-century script loops in extravagant curves
rendering each capital-letter as ornate as a Restoration brooch.

The city reeks of oldness. The sense of decrepitude takes me by surprise, not only in the cemeteries but on all
of the narrow and cobbled streets. This is the new world, but the ground itself feels old and resentful. I feel
like it will rise up and spit me out because my feet don't belong here. I feel the ripples will chase me across the
world in an earthquake of resentment. In one cemetery I find all the puritans you could ever wish for: four
theologians buried smugly alongside the lopsided headstone of a so-called adulteress called Elizabeth Pain.
She was tried for infanticide, found not guilty, but never the less flogged and cast out. Pain seems such a good name for a woman buried among puritans.

Everywhere in this gloom Stars and Stripes hang hunched like closed-winged-moths on poles propped against
patriot graves. A ground full of founding fathers buried in a place where light seldom visits. Flag after flag
pitched in damp air to remind a patchwork-nation of immigrants that this is where you live and this is who you
are. Let no one else follow you in. Wear your red cap and close the gates. Fly those American flags, some green
with mould, some thinned by time and falling apart.

This is America.
This is where America was made.
In this graveyard.

Ukraine: the Farmer's Daughter

Diane Cockburn

When you told her,
I ran out into the fields and lay down in the wheat.
I covered my eyes and ears in gold because that way
I did not need to hear the message you brought.
Your words had torn down all the telephone wires.
I could not call you back to check.
The birds had exploded into silence.
So, what was there to do?
Just lie and watch the clouds come.
The edges of the fields so neat they held us
tight in a quilt of golden wheat;
the grey sky muffling around our heads,
until we shouted.
No respite from the cold gold glare of the metal fields.
No harvest.
No soft bread.
Not this year.

The Women Wait

Meghana Karanjkar

They wait,
As they have been told to, made to, suffragetted to
And again, they are defeated
Told they are not good or good enough
The women wait

Even when
They are imprisoned, raped and burnt
Again and again, over and over
Shown their place in the world
The women wait

The oval office hollow
Their seat at the table empty
Their stricken voices muffled
The power of the feminine dimmed
The women wait

While they bear children, tend house and feed husbands
Again and again, over and over
Their bodies not theirs
While they nurture, nourish and raise
The women wait

Unnurtured, unnourished and unloved
Yet again we rise, we fight, we die
For our voice
Our bodies
For control, over our own fate.

Silenced

Caroline Dowse

The café is often warm at this time of day. Today, it is almost unbearable. I listen to our husbands talking, their voices washing over me like water.

My sister and I don't talk, at least not in public. We remember our father's words:

it's safer that way.

A vehicle pulls up outside, and the talking stops. The door opens and three men enter. Machine guns.

Army fatigues.

I look away.

It's safer that way.

The thud of boots on the floor is followed by the scraping of a chair as someone is hauled to their feet.

No. Two people.

I chance a look. It's the couple in the corner. Two of the soldiers march them to the door, where the third waits. The captured man protests, but it is hopeless. He must realise. The woman does. She stays silent.

They are escorted out by the two soldiers, but the third remains. His eyes rake across each of us, as if daring us to protest. Perhaps he wants a reaction, but he won't get one.

It's safer that way.

I cast my eyes to the floor and focus on his boots. They are dirty, scuffed brown with mud. They have walked the streets a lot, those boots. Where else have they been? How many others have seen them, and followed their heavy tread outside?

I can feel my lungs expanding, like I'm about to scream. My vision blurs, and my breathing is ragged. I try to calm myself, breathe deeply.

Not here.

Not in front of him.

It's not safe.

Someone grabs my thigh, sharp nails digging into my flesh through my clothes. The pain jolts me, bringing me back to myself, and the scream dies within me. I glance at my sister and incline my head slightly.

Thank you.

She releases her grip, and I return my gaze to the floor.

I hear the heavy tread of the soldier's boots heading towards the door, and the tinkle of the bell as it opens and closes. Everybody holds their breath, waiting for the vehicle to leave. Once its engine is nothing but a distant hum, the men resume their conversation.

My sister and I look at each other, a shared look of relief.

It wasn't us – this time.

The tears will come later, I am sure.

But that can wait until I am alone.

It's safer that way.

This, in our blood

Mona Dash

we laugh so hard that our mouths turn inwards and lose shape
then paint smiles on, upturned scars, watch poppy fields turn blue
we dream of faraway lands where the flowers are red and fragrant
with peacocks and poems and picture-books and forests verdant

the song humming inside remains one of sadness
of something beautiful, breaking in a flash
a lover leaving mid-kiss on a sunlit evening in Venice city of water
bleeding, oozing, weeping sores even years after

memories rush back to bite; in the waves that come and go
shoals of sprat leap, fall, then die on our feet
even as we watch, even as the water trickles from under our toes
we are voiceless, eyes morose, vacant in our many faces

the abyss inside, the one outside, a desolate seascape mirror
deep down, the sadness in us, in our blood, our skin, our bones
reaches the skies in a whirling column, boomerang-like pirouettes
back towards us, as we sob; we sob, fragments of ash and vapour.

Poem for Karen in Heavy Times

Joonna Smitherman Trapp

Thick heavy air, dense with cloud
obscures ends of tree limbs which poke
upward into misty nothingness.
But cacophony of birdsong lightly floats
down from humidity
reminding
that something is.
The nothingness is not all.

How Hope Is Made

Lois Perch Villemaire

Hope is designed in the mind,
a collage of positive images pasted
with chocolate chips and confetti.
It begins with a dream, not in sleep
but during waking hours
as you venture to the outer edges
of a rose garden in bloom.
Hope is a reflection
of an untamed imagination,
expectations come true.
Hope is sustained with
blueberry muffins and sunlight,
dandelions and a tablespoon
of peanut butter. When hope is lost
look beyond the foggy morning,
visualize a bright orange sunset,
a pumpkin nearing the horizon.
Encourage hope to return
with promises of walks on the beach.
Welcome hope with hugs and love,
comfort hope with hot cocoa
and nutty banana bread.
Keep hope alive by propagating joy
from a single leaf of your being.

Irises

Gillie Griffin

March. The geese flying home to breed.
Two large Vs intersect in the sky above my garden.
I watch them taking turns to fall back,
drifting behind the tail of the leader.
I want to call out "Careful now, look out for each other",
remembering the year so many flew at once.
Crashed bodies fell from the sky,
feathers and carcasses across the highway.

March. White storks migrating home to nest.
Large flocks of hungry birds over Gaza,
searching for places to rest, to feed. I want to call to them.
"Don't stop. No fields here will yield you grain."
"Fly on, fly high above the bombing."
"No radar will track your flight, nor keep your passage
safe this year."

Fly on to the Gilboa mountains where nothing moves
and everything changes. Rocks ground down by the wind
particles of blue sand blown elsewhere,
seeds transported by birds, by air, by animals' feet,
finding pockets of soil to settle, reclaiming a right to flourish.

March. On Gilboa neither dew nor rain,
yet the irises are blooming.
Tissue paper petals, a frilly transparency,
fully at odds with the land. Wounded shades of blue and purple,
yellow and brown. A living bruise.
Not a cat's lick of moisture anywhere.

March. In my garden
Blue-green blades of irises split
the frozen ground. As if they haven't heard
it's minus four this morning. Wind blowing
a good howl. Threats of drifting snow.
As if they are saying "Bring it on."
It will be months until they flower. Spring dreams

long stored underground.
As if they are saying "Throw anything. We intend to survive."

Wren

Melanie Higgs

Her littleness
Belittles winter.
Tweaking fate
In my garden
One seed at a time
She pricks the snow
Beneath the feeder,
A dainty jackhammer.

I've turned off the news,
Helpless.
There is no smaller way to feel.

I watch another
Alight, bob and dip
Around the first.
She flicks a seed over.
They move on.

They have discovered a tiny fish that makes the noise of a jackhammer

Rachel Burns

somewhere in Myanmar,
a place where people are fleeing

to escape military conscription
which reminds me of Stefan,

who came to live with us
that summer, hop-picking,

to avoid joining the German military
& there was never enough hot water.

I think he's married now with a daughter,
& the shower is broken again,

my husband says he can't fix it.
I have to fill a jug with water,

which is to say, sometimes,
I feel like a daughter of Danaus,

the water jug full of holes
everything an impossibility.

& later travelling to work,
the woman on the train

in the silent carriage,
playing a loud grating video game

& at the same time
talking incessantly into her phone

which is to say, I sometimes find myself,

on the wrong train, travelling backwards.

Doll Houses

Nancy Shattuck

Watching black smoke billow from the high rise
where Russians have bombed Ukrainians
to expose one more doll house view
of rooms with one wall stripped away,

I see the remains of a life lived within:
beds, couches, chair still in place
though covered with slivered glass shards,
the flimsiest furnishings ruined sticks.

There an old man shakes out a blanket
and folds it, salvaging, like Linus
what we called a "security blanket"
in our Sunday comic strips.
Now, even knowing it's a landmine,
A ruined hair shirt,
I want to wrap it around him.

Evening Primrose

Avril Joy

Sunday 10th November 2025, Donald Trump is elected to the Presidency of the
USA for the second time

I go out
unknown, leaving
my cocoon, the echo chamber
I spun for myself, this feathered thing
of podcasts and You Tubes.

Patient on the table, mask on mouth
I go out
unsure what day it is
except it is the day after the election
cloud grey morning and only the barest

glimpse of sun through gauze.
In the two-horse field the horses' heads
bowed, back blanketed, breath smoke
I go out
looking for consolation.

In the grass on the church path
a solitary stem of evening primrose
only three petals remaining
barely a flower
it stands defiant –

sun-drop, fever plant,
cure-all –
antidote to bruise and wound
taken by women for pain in the breast
small, yellow star of hope.

Solitary Bee

Kathryn Jordan

Three days in the house of my old father.
He sits, hunched over, thumbing pages of

a piece written to honor him, determined
to point out mistakes. I offer an apology.

He says, *Are you sorry for what you did*
or that you wrote it? Then, *You know what*

I think. I take the bait: "Why isn't this over?"
My father is silent, still scrolling my work.

I go to my room, consider the cost to fly
home today. Through a dark glass, I see

a bee hovering at the open window, which
I rush to close to a crack, lest a bug enter

or—God forbid—a wild, fresh prairie wind.
The bee lands near a hole in the lock, starts

to dig, tiny legs tugging at tiny bits of web
and shit, squeezing its body into an opening

scarcely larger than itself, emerging to kick
away traces of clinging, clotted matter. She

flies off, returning to clear the space inside
over and over. Does she never tire of this?

The sun goes down behind still-bare trees,
washing the prairie of light. All is hushed

and calm, though I don't know what changed.
I crouch by the window, peering out, hoping

she can rest, solitary bee, hidden in her cave.

Nesting

Chris Baral

I curl up like a ball of yarn
afraid that if I stand
I might
Unravel.

If hope is the thing with feathers
then let me fly away

but when the world brings wear and tear
even birds seek refuge
they join in molt migrations
to keep their feathers strong

when songbirds molt
they do not sing
nor do they fly
too vulnerable
they must find rest
until feathered
once again.

Today I came upon a nest
where seeming strands
of spun gold thread
instead, were lengths of caution tape
unraveled
in the twigs.

What Keeps Me

Pamela Bordisso

During this time of unraveling
I step through the garden gate

Amidst chaos and pain I surrender
into the embrace of new collard greens

Evenly planted from the plastic pack
bright against dark compost

This vibrant composition
smell of earth, makes life bearable

Tastes of coming meals wave
in the breeze, my spine lengthens

Garden nurturance
Keeps me upright

Heather

Angie Athanassiades

The dry duff crackles as
I walk through the forest,
the desiccation of summer
persisting like insidious grief,

the process of autumn
forced to a standstill.

Everything is dying —

rosemary bushes brittle,
burnt brown, the drops
of the first rain sliding
off the dead leaves
like an apology
offered too late,

tortoises scrambling
in the damp dust searching
for the grass that won't grow —
not yet, not in time for their long
sleep — flattening the few cyclamen
that gave false hope weeks ago.

The heather knew, sending
forth its first leaves cautiously
only after the air turned cold,
not a day early, and even then,
its fine, silver stems held on
to what life was left inside

them, rationing the leaves as
they appeared one by one,
day by day.

Today, as the first rain falls
through the forest, the heather

is ready to receive it, its few
shy leaves reaching out
to welcome it in their best
new green.

Maybe in a few days purple
and pink flowers will appear,
will be held by the stems
that suffered the heat of summer
with this one purpose,

by the leaves that, arresting the course
of unassuming raindrops,
sent the scant water to the parched
earth covering their roots.

I no longer look to the dying
rosemary for guidance, or
to the tortoises scrambling
about like blind prophets;

I crouch down and sit
by the heather, my hands
held out like leaves catching
what they can of hope.

I follow Mary Oliver
and make my way to the water's edge

Nelly Bryce

I follow Mary Oliver,
and make my way to the water's edge.

I do not fall but rather unfurl – my fingers
then each vein of my breath like a fern.
I unfold out of myself
until the leaves of my body find space to rest.

Here, by the water
all 'this' and 'that' is irrelevant.
The ground beneath me is a gift,
the smell of the ground is a welcome home.

Here, I am able to feel what I have always known.
I will stay as long as I can bare the cold and
then I will stay longer still.
I will swim under the dark night of this moon.

Here, the water makes its way on and on,
the quiet rush
of my ever hopeful mind.

They executed me on a bright afternoon in February

Rebecca Faulkner
for Sophie Scholl, 1921-1943

& the sky was silent as my brother wept
Thousands among us dissent
but the sun is weary & does not wait
Gestapo at our throats scream
high treason, perspire in empty
corridors at the knife edge of defeat, flirt
with a cowardly mob who close
their ears to the crack of a blade brisk as air
meeting skin, who continue to shop & drink
& fuck on such a fine sunny day
Who among us is ashamed? My skull
severed cleanly with spring crouching low
Hair knotted in the stocks, my words
rush forward, catching the light

Awash

Amrita Skye Blaine

I don't watch
yet I'm awash
in headlines, snippets
of gossip at the store
yet another executive order
Sharpie-signed,
a stuttering electro-
cardiogram
cutting this, closing that
oops! nope, roll it back

allies gobsmacked
foes sniggering
citizens baffled
by his slashing sword

for peace of heart
I ramble Blackberry Lane
noting songbirds' rustle
clouds forming,
dissolving
Acacia's resin scent
redolent of spring

New dawn

Khadija Rouf

Last day here, for some time to come.
Drinking coffee and looking out one more time

The sunlight travelling across the mountains
The soft shadows scudding after

Boats lullaby, swaying in the loch
A solitary gull perches on a chimney pot

All this ordinary is delicious to my eyes
So there is sadness in knowing

Everything looks the same
But stars have unspangled

Today
Everything is changed...so

I must change too; spark ignition, become us,
Fan into blue wings, make and share light.

Poets

ANGIE ATHANASSIADES

Angie Athanassiades writes poetry, memoir and lyric essays. Her work has appeared in *Serving House Journal* and KYSO flash. Her essays *Boats Against the Current* and *The Antikythera Shipwreck* were nominated for the Best of the Net award and the Pushcart Prize respectively. Her memoir, *I am Twig, Bone, Feather*, will be published by Vine Leaves Press in April 2026. She lives in Greece and is inspired by nature, mythology and migrating birds.

CHRIS BARAL

Chris Baral is a lifelong poet whose writing focuses on nature and politics. She lived in the SF Bay Area for many years before settling in the Berkshires in Western Massachusetts where she serves on the conservation committee for the town of Egremont. She works at Husch Vineyards, a regeneratively farmed winery located in Anderson Valley in Mendocino CA and writes poetry whenever she can. She finds inspiration and balance during very early morning kayak rides. Her poem, "Fractals" was selected to be included in the print anthology of The Nature of Our Times: Poems on America's Lands, Waters, Wildlife and Other Natural Wonders (due in September 2025 from Paloma Press, in collaboration with Wick Poetry Center at Kent State University and Poets for Science).

ELLEN BASS

Ellen Bass's most recent collection is *Indigo* (Copper Canyon Press, 2020). Among her awards are Fellowships from the Guggenheim Foundation, the NEA, the Lambda Literary Award, and four Pushcart Prizes. She co-edited the first major anthology of women's poetry, *No More Masks*. A Chancellor Emerita of the Academy of American Poets, Bass teaches in Pacific University's MFA program.

LAURA BISSELL

Laura Bissell is a writer, researcher and arts educator from Glasgow. Laura's writing has been published in Gutter, *New Writing Scotland*, *Tip Tap Flat*, *The Edwin Morgan Centenary Collection* and *From Glasgow to Saturn* amongst others. Laura is author of *A-Z of Sites of Love and Loss*, *Bubbles: Reflections on Becoming Mother* and guest edited the poetry collection *Things there are no words for*.

AMRITA SKYE BLAINE

Amrita Skye Blaine develops themes of impermanence, aging, disability, and awakening. Her first collection of poetry, *strange grace—the ending season*, poems on impermanence, aging and death, is newly available on Amazon. Her second collection, *every riven thing*, was just published by Finishing Line Press.

PAMELA BORDISSO

Pamela Bordisso is a poet in Kelseyville, California. She lives in a rural area under massive oaks. She tends chickens, bees, vegetables, and plants for pollinators. She has been published in Last Stanza Journal, Colussus:Body, Noyo Review, and the Lake County Bloom. She fights despair with action. Some days it's writing postcards, calling politicians, other days it's growing flowers or writing a poem.

NELLY BRYCE

Nelly Bryce is a writer, poet and mother of four from Manchester, UK. She published her first book of poetry, 'Motherhood Minus the Medals' in 2022 and is currently writing her second. She's an enthusiastic 'feminist killjoy' and journaling addict who is big on feelings. She runs a poetry book club and community on Substack called Poetry Pals.

RACHEL BURNS

Rachel Burns is published in literary magazines including *14 Magazine*, *Butcher's Dog*, *The Rialto*, *Ink, Sweat and Tears*, *Atrium*, *The Friday Poem*, *Magma*, and *The London Magazine*. Her poetry pamphlet, *A Girl in a Blue Dress*, is published by Vane Women Press, and her first collection is forthcoming with Broken Sleep Books. Socials: X @RachelLBurnsme, INSTA rachelburns3224

REGI CLAIRE

Swiss-born Regi Claire won the Mslexia/PBS Poetry Competition 2019 and was shortlisted for the Forward Prizes 2020 (Best Single Poem). Her poems have appeared in *Acumen*, *Ambit*, *Antigonish Review*, *Best New British & Irish Poets*, *Best Scottish Poems*, *New European*, *Rialto*, *Southword*, *Stand*, *Under the Radar* and others. Her fiction has won a UBS Cultural Foundation award and twice been shortlisted for Scotland's National Book Awards. She is a Teaching Fellow at Edinburgh University. www.regiclaire.com

DIANE COCKBURN

Diane Cockburn is a Northern Irish poet living and working in Durham. Brought up in Belfast, she find echoes in myth and folklore, often using dark humour to make sense of an unsettling world. She has an MA in Poetry from Northumbria University and is published in a range of anthologies, magazines, and online. Her latest collection Electric Mermaid is published by Arrowhead Press. She has just completed a new collection of poetry.

MONA DASH

Mona Dash is an award-winning author based in London. Her work includes her memoir *A Roll of the Dice*, a short story collection *Let Us Look Elsewhere*, a novel *Untamed Heart* and two collections of poetry, *A Certain Way* and *Dawn Drops*. Her work has been presented on BBC Radio 4, included in Best British Short Stories, and published in more than thirty-five anthologies. She is represented by Portobello Literary. Her next poetry collection *Map of the Self* is forthcoming from Linen Press in October 2025. She also works as a business leader in AI for a global tech company. More details at www.monadash.net or follow her on Instagram at monadash_

CAROLINE DOWSE

Caroline Dowse is a creative writing graduate from Peterborough. Currently, she writes articles for *The Publishing Post* and The Lower Tiers, a football news website. In her spare time, she volunteers in her local library and is a Literacy Champion for the National Literacy Trust in Peterborough.

ALEXIS RHONE FANCHER

Alexis Rhone Fancher is published in *Best American Poetry*, *Rattle*, *The American Journal of Poetry*, *Spillway*, *Plume*, *Diode*, *The Pedestal Magazine*, *Duende*, *Vox Populi*, *Gargoyle*, *Elysium Review*, and elsewhere. She's authored eleven poetry collections, most recently, *TRIGGERED*, (MacQueens) and *BRAZEN*, (NYQ). A multi Pushcart Prize and Best of the net nominee, Alexis recently won Best MicroFictions, 2025. She calls the Mojave Desert home.

REBECCA FAULKNER

Rebecca Faulkner is a London-born poet based in Brooklyn. She is the author of *Permit Me to Write My Own Ending*, (Write Bloody Publishing, 2023) which was a finalist for the 2024 Sheila Margaret Motton Book Prize. Her work appears in *New York Quarterly*, *The Maine Review*, *The Poetry Society of New York*, *CALYX Press*, *Berkeley Poetry Review* and elsewhere. Her new collection, Daughters of the Minotaur, engages with the life and work of five mid-century women artists, and is forthcoming in 2027 from Regal House Publishing. www.rebeccafaulknerpoet.com

MARA GALE FEIN

Mara Gale Fein most often writes of loss. Her work will appear shortly in *Contemporary Haibun Online* and can also be found in *California Quarterly*, *Amethyst Review*, *Tahoma Literary Review*, and *Poor Yorick*, among others. She resides in Los Angeles and received a doctorate in English from the University of Southern California.

GILLIE GRIFFIN

Gillie Griffin moved to Canada from the UK in 1994. Along with one husband, one dog and one cat, she lives in the village of Wakefield, Québec on the unceded traditional territories of the Algonquin/Anishinabeg peoples, where she co-hosts "Poetea" a monthly poetry reading series. Since 2021, she has lived a "re-wired" life, still working on issues related to animal research ethics, but spending more time as Nana to three grandkids, writing, and talking to the plants in her garden. She has published one book of poems *Warm Bodies: Foreign Parts* with Loxwood-Stonleigh press, and was included in the Linen Press Anthology *Tabula Rasa* in 2023.

NICOLE GULOTTA

Nicole Gulotta is the author of *Wild Words: Rituals, Routines, and Rhythms for Braving the Writer's Path* and *Eat This Poem: A Literary Feast of Recipes Inspired by Poetry*. To connect with her podcast or newsletter, visit nicolemgulotta.com.

MARE HERON HAKE

Mare Heron Hake (she/her) is a poet of the South Salish Sea region, Puget Sound, in Washington State. With her MFA, Hake has been a poetry editor, co-owner, and co-publisher for Tahoma Literary Review before her care-giving responsibilities took precedence. Work has appeared for Terrain.Org, the Atlanta Review, other journals and publications, as well as *Duo*, published by Linen Press. Still surprising to her, she has two books available through Amazon.

MELANIE HIGGS

Melanie Higgs lives on the unceded territory of the Halkomelem people on Vancouver Island, Canada. She won Honourable Mention for her poem, 'Brigid's Gift' in the Victoria Writers' Society Contest in 2021. Her poetry has appeared in the *Island Writer Magazine* and has been anthologized in *Word and Vision* (Cowichan Valley Arts Council), *Worth More Standing* (Caitlin Press & Dagger Editions), and *Tabula Rasa*, (Linen Press). She will never get used to the thrill of choosing one word after another in what she hopes is just the right order.

CONNIE HILLS

Connie Hills grew up in the southwest corner of the USA. After working as a Psychologist for thirty years, she retired her clinical practice to devote her time to writing poetry. Her poems have appeared in journals such as *Porter Gulch Review*, *Red Rock Review*, *Red Wheelbarrow Literary Magazine*, *Bark*, *San Diego Poetry Annual*, and *Catamaran*. She is a pushcart nominee. Connie resides in San Francisco - in the Pacific Ocean's abundant natural light - with her wife and their curious whippet.

KAVITA A. JINDAL

Kavita A. Jindal is a poet, novelist and essayist. Her most recent publication is *The Planet Spins On Its Axis, Regardless*, a short story collection. Her poetry volumes include *Patina* and *Raincheck Renewed*. Her novel *Manual For A Decent Life* won the Eastern Eye Award for Fiction. www.kavitajindal.com

KATHRYN JORDAN

Kathryn Jordan is the winner of the San Miguel de Allende Writers Conference Prize for Poetry. Her work has won awards in the Steve Kowit, Muriel Craft Bailey, Connecticut Poetry, Sidney Lanier, Patricia Dobler and Cantor poetry contests and has been published widely. *Solitary Bee* won Honorable Mention in the Connecticut Poetry Award, 2024. She loves to hike the trails, listening for birdsong to transcribe to poems. http://kathrynjordan.org/

AVRIL JOY

Avril Joy is a novelist, short story writer and poet. Her work has been shortlisted in competitions including the Bridport and the Manchester Prize for Fiction. Her poetry has appeared in the *Forward Prize* anthology. In 2012 her short story, *Millie and Bird*, won the inaugural Costa Short Story Award. Her novel, *Sometimes a River Song* won the 2017 People's Book Prize. Her latest novel from publisher Linen Press is *The Silent Women*.

MEGHANA KARANJKAR

Meghana Karanjkaris a short story writer as well as a non-fiction essayist and a poet. She has recently completed her first book of short stories. A few of her stories and essays have been published in *The Adelaide Journal*, *The Blue Mountain Review* and elsewhere. Meghana is a BIPOC first generation immigrant and her writing is informed by this experience. She lives in New Jersey, USA, with her family and a big, yellow Lab.

LINDSAY KELLAR-MADSEN

Lindsay Kellar-Madsen is a Canadian writer who scribbles compulsively in rare sleeves of time. She lives in the Danish countryside with her husband and four children, who only wear shoes when necessary. Her poems appear in *The Shore*, *Blue* by Humana Obscura, *Sugared Water* by Porkbelly Press, *Green Ink*, and *Snapdragon Journal*. She is the author of two children's books: *Meet the Wild* (2023) and *The Lovely Haze of Baby Days* (2021), published by Little Otter Press. Learn more at: www.lindsaykmadsen.com

SUSAN BRADY KONIG

Susan Brady Konig is the New York-based author of three books on motherhood: *Why Animals Sleep So Close to the Road (and Other Lies I Tell My Children)*, *I Wear the Maternity Pants in This Family*, and *Teenagers & Toddlers Are Trying to Kill Me!* Her piece in this anthology is from *Just Fine in Paris*, a yet-to-be-published memoir on grief and identity.

JOAN LEOTTA

Joan Leotta plays with words on page and stage. She's been published as an essayist, poet, short story writer, and novelist. She's a two-time nominee for Pushcart and Best of the Net. Her poetry, essays, and stories have appeared in *The Ekphrastic Review*, *The Lake*, *Ovunque Siamo*, *One Art*, *Gargoyle*, and other journals. She's taught in Northern VA Community College, Brunswick County Arts Council, North Dakota Humanities Program. Her shows most often highlight her Italian heritage, food, family, and strong women and has been a guest on British (Tony Cranston's program) and Italian radio (Radio Cavolo). Her new one-woman show is "Louisa May Alcott".

S. J. LITHERLAND

S. J. Litherland has eight published collections, the latest *Marginal Future* and *Composition in White* both from Smokestack Books. She lives in Durham, a founder member of North East writing, performing and publishing collective Vane Women. Two Northern Arts Awards and twice won Commendations in the National Poetry Competition.

CAROL MCKAY

Carol McKay's poetry, fiction and creative non-fiction have been published widely for over 25 years. Awards include the Robert Louis Stevenson Fellowship. Her website is https://carolmckay.co.uk

SALLY J. MORGAN

Sally J. Morgan is Welsh born and a dual British and New Zealand citizen. Winner of the 2022 Portico Prize for *Toto Among the Murderers* (John Murray Press), Sally was longlisted for the NZ Jann Medicott Acorn Prize for Fiction, and shortlisted for the Hubert Church Prize for Best First Work of Fiction in 2021. She has been published in *Landfall Literary Journal*, the *Guardian*, the *Irish Times*, *The Spinoff*, *International Journal of Heritage Studies*, *Journal of Historical Geography*, *European Journal of Cultural Studies*, *Journal of Visual Arts Practice*, *Act: Writing Art* and others.

SUE MOULES

Walking the Whippet was chosen for 2024 Brighton and Hove *Poems on the Buses*. *Poems in By Ways Anthology* (Arachne) 2024 and *Words on Troubled Waters* (Lutra Press) 2024. Her most recent collection is *The Moth Box* (Parthian).

NANCY SHATTUCK

Nancy Shattuck is the author of three historical fiction novels posed against the background of 1676 King Philip's War in Massachusetts. These begin her inquiry into the indigenous warriors' side in the conflict, and she continues her examination in the three new books plotted in the series "The Watertown Chronicles." She lives in the Detroit Metropolitan area where she edits Indy works and teaches Memoir.

JESS RICHARDS

Jess Richards is the author of three literary fiction novels: Costa shortlisted *Snake Ropes*, *Cooking with Bones*, and *City of Circles* (Sceptre). Her latest book is *Birds and Ghosts*, a work of creative nonfiction (Linen Press).

KHADIJA ROUF

Khadija Rouf has published in magazines such as *Orbis, Six Seasons, Sarasvati* and *DreamCatcher*. Her poems appear in the 2020 NHS anthology, *These are the Hands* (Fair Acre Press). Her collection *HouseWork* is also published by Fair Acre Press (2022). She is also a member of The Whole Kahani whose anthology, *Tongues and Bellies* is published by Linen Press (2021). Her work has appeared in *Tabula Rasa* (2022) also published by Linen Press. She is a regular reviewer for *The Friday Poem*.

ANNIE TALBOT

Annie Talbot has been writing poetry and fiction since she was seven years old. She spent several years living in foreign countries with her family and has deep empathy for others who do the same. She now lives in California, with her husband, teenager and their dog.

ABIGAIL THOMAS

Abigail Thomas's poems and prose have been published in *The Paris Review*, *The Nation*, *The Missouri Review*, and elsewhere. She is the author of the memoirs: *Safekeeping, A Three Dog Life, What Comes Next* and *How To Like it* and most recently, *Still Life at Eighty*. She has four children, twelve grandchildren, two great-grandchildren, eleven books, and a high school education.

JOONNA SMITHERMAN TRAPP

Joonna Smitherman Trapp has served as a department chair at several colleges. She and her colleagues founded the first Writing Program at Emory University. Recently retired, she is working on several writing projects, including her poetry. Her book manuscript is under contract and revision; it examines the 19th century Lyceum movement in the Old South and its impact on literacy and communication education.

LOIS PERCH VILLEMAIRE
Lois Perch Villemaire of Annapolis, MD is the author of *My Eight Greats* (2023) and *Eyes at the Edge of the Woods* (Bottlecap Press 2024). Her poetry has appeared in *Spillwords Press*, *The RavensPerch*, *Third Street Review*, and elsewhere. Her flash memoir has been included in anthologies including "I Am My Father's Daughter." She is a contributing writer to AARP The Ethel. Lois, a Pushcart nominee researches genealogy, volunteers at the library, and propagates African violets.

JESS WATTS
Jess Watts lives and writes in South London. She is the author of *The Sun-Room: a prose poem memoir about chronic illness grief*, published April 2025 by Linen Press. jesswattsauthor.com

BETH OAST WILLIAMS
Beth Oast Williams is the author of the chapbook *Riding Horses in the Harbor* (Finishing Line Press, 2020). Her poetry has been accepted for publication in *Nimrod*, *Salamander*, Leon *Literary Review*, *SWWIM*, *One Art*, *Dialogist*, *Invisible City* and *Rattle's Poets Respond*, among others, and nominated twice for the Pushcart Prize.

ANDRENA ZAWINSKI
Andrena Zawinski is an American poet whose poetry has received accolades for free verse, form, lyricism, spirituality, and social concern. Her book of poetry, *Traveling in Reflected Light*, was a Kenneth Patchen competition winner. *Something About* received a PEN Oakland Josephine Miles Award for Excellence in Literature. Her third full-length collection is *Landings* and fourth is *Born Under the Influence*. Originally from Pittsburgh, Pennsylvania, she makes her home in the San Francisco Bay Area in California.

Acknowledgements

Ellen Bass's *Laundry, Lighthouse and Pale Blue Vein.*
Laundry was originally published in *The New Yorker*, April 29, 2024. *Lighthouse* was originally published in *You Are Here: Poetry in the Natural World*, ed. Ada Limón (Milkweed Editions, 2024) *Pale Blue Vein* was originally published in *Narrative Magazine* (Winter, 2024).

Diane Cockburn's *Ukraine* will be published in her new poetry collection, provisionally to be launched in early September 2025 with Mudfog Press.

Alexis Rhone Fancher's *Suicide des Oiseaux: The Apocalypse* was published in *Book of Matches*, Winter 2025. Alexis is the author of ten books of poetry, most recently BRAZEN (New York Quarterly), and TRIGGERED (MacQueen's Press). Her photo portrait book of over 100 Southern California poets publishes in early 2026 from Moon Tide Press. Find her at: www.alexisrhonefancher.com

Rebecca Faulkner's *Fireweed* was first published in Faulkner's collection, Permit Me to Write My Own Ending. *They executed me on a bright afternoon in February* was first published by Into the Void and is included in Permit Me to Write My Own Ending.

Joan Leotta's *Spotting a Splash of Red* was first published by Lothlorien Poetry Journal in September 2024.

Nancy Shattuck's *Doll Houses* has been previously published in an anthology *Silence is Consent* edited by Christopher Bogrt, Casablanca Press, 2025.

Jess Richards's Watching *Perfume Ads with the Sound Off* was first published in the *Aesthetica Creative Writing Awards Anthology*, 2025. (Aesthetica Magazine Ltd.)

Lois Villemaire's *How Hope Is Made* was previously published in *Flora Fiction Literary Magazine* Vol 4 Issue 4.

Andrena Zawinski's *Anchorless in the Light* was previously published in *Light on the Walls of Life Tribute Anthology to Lawrence Ferlinghetti* (2021) and appears in the book by the author, *Born Under the Influence* (2022).